SCHIRMER'S LIBRARY
OF MUSICAL CLASSICS

Vol. 2071

LUDVIG VAN BEETHOVEN

Favorite Piano Works

10 Sonatas, 3 Variations, 4 Sonatinas

10 Bagatelles, 8 Other Pieces

ISBN 978-1-4234-3129-9

G. SCHIRMER, Inc.

DISTRIBUTED BY

HAL•LEONARD®
CORPORATION
7777 W. BLUEMOUND RD. P.O. BOX 13819 MILWAUKEE, WI 53213

www.schirmer.com
www.halleonard.com

CONTENTS

SONATAS

VARIATIONS

SONATINAS

BAGATELLES

VARIOUS PIECES

Dedicated to Joseph Haydn

SONATA
in F minor

Edited by Carl Krebs

Ludwig van Beethoven
Op. 2, No. 1

MENUETTO.
Allegretto.

Dedicated to Countess von Browne

SONATA
in C minor

Edited by Carl Krebs

Ludwig van Beethoven
Op. 10, No. 1

23

Adagio molto.

25

FINALE.
Prestissimo.

SONATA
in F Major

Edited by Carl Krebs

Ludwig van Beethoven
Op. 10, No. 2

Allegretto.

Presto.

SONATA
in C minor
"Pathétique"

Edited by Carl Krebs

Ludwig van Beethoven
Op. 13

attacca subito il Allegro.

44

Allegro di molto e con brio.

46

Tempo I.

Allegro molto e con brio.

attacca subito Allegro molto e con brio.

Adagio cantabile.

RONDO
Allegro.

Dedicated to Baroness von Braun

SONATA
in E Major

Edited by Carl Krebs

Ludwig van Beethoven
Op. 14, No. 1

Maggiore

66

D.c.Allegretto e poi la Coda.

Coda.

RONDO.
Allegro commodo.

Dedicated to Baroness von Braun

SONATA
in G Major

Edited by Carl Krebs

Ludwig van Beethoven
Op. 14, No. 2

Andante.
La prima parte senza replica.

SCHERZO.
Allegro assai.

Dedicated to Countess Julie Guicciardi

SONATA
in C-sharp minor
(Quasi una Fantasia)
"Moonlight"

Edited by Carl Krebs

Ludwig van Beethoven
Op. 27, No. 2

Adagio sostenuto.
Si deve suonare tutto questo pezzo delicatissimamente e senza sordino.

sempre **pp** e senza sordino

Allegretto.
La prima parte senza repetizione.

Trio.

Presto agitato.

Allegretto da capo.

(This page has been intentionally left blank.)

SONATA
in G minor

Edited and fingered by
Sigmund Lebert and Hans von Bülow

Ludwig van Beethoven
Op. 49, No. 1

Abbreviations: M. T., signifies Main Theme; S. T., Sub Theme; Cl. T., Closing Theme; D. G., Development-group;
R., Return; Tr., Transition; Md. T., Mid-Theme; Ep., Episode; App., Appendix.

a) *mfp* signifies: the first note *mf*, the following ones *p*.

b) With the comma we indicate places where the player must perceptibly mark the end of a rhythmic group or section, by lifting the last note just before its time-value expires, although the composer wrote no rest.

c)

d) The left hand more subdued than the right, but still accenting the first of each pair of 16th-notes (i. e.: the bass notes proper) somewhat more than the second.

e)

f) Here and in the next measure the left hand should accent only the first note in each group of 16th-notes somewhat more than the others, but in all cases less than the soprano.

g) As at d.)

h) In these three measures as at f.)

a) As at (f) on the preceding Page.

b)

c) The left hand here again more subdued than the right.

d) As at (a).

e) In these twelve measures the first and third notes in each group of 16th notes should be made somewhat more prominent than the other notes, yet always in subordination to the melody, excepting the tones marked ＞

a) From here through the next 6 measures the left hand, having the melody, should predominate over the right, and, where it has 2 tones, chiefly accentuate the higher one.

b) As on first Page.

c) The next 5 measures as on first Page.

d) Doubtless literally meant neither for ♪♪♪♪ nor for: ♪♪♪♪ but ♪♪♪♪

e) This and the following turns again as on first Page.

f) From here onward as on second Page.

Rondo.
Allegro. (♩.= 92.)

a) sf

b) a tempo

a)

b) Proceed only after a rest.

a) In these groups of 16th-notes, accent each first note slightly more than the 5 following, while subordinating all to the soprano. These same accented notes, too, (except in the fourth measure) should be held down during the second 16th-note.

b) Also subordinate this accompaniment, but accent the first note of each triplet, as the bass note proper, a trifle more than the other two.

a)

b) Here, of course, only the first eighth-note in each measure should be accented.

a) From here up to the *ff* discreetly subordinate the left hand throughout (also in the repetitions of the fundamental tone.)
b) Let the *ff* enter abruptly with the fourth eighth-note, without any previous *crescendo*.

SONATA
in G Major

Edited and fingered by
Sigmund Lebert and Hans von Bülow

Ludwig van Beethoven
Op. 49, No. 2

Abbreviations: M.T. signifies Main Theme; S.T., Sub-Theme; Cl.T., Closing Theme; D.G., Development-Group; R., Return; Tr., Transition; Md.T. Mid-Theme; Ep., Episode.

Allegro ma non troppo. ($\quad$ = 132.)

a) Strike all short **appoggiaturas** on the beat, simultaneously with the accompaniment-note.

b) F♯ should be executed as a long, accented **appoggiatura**:

a) ♫♫♫ easier: ♫♫♫

112

Tempo di Menuetto. (♩ = 112.)

a) *mp* (*mezzo piano*, moderately soft) signifies a degree of tone-power midway between *p* and *mf*.

SONATA
in G Major

Edited and fingered by
Sigmund Lebert and Hans von Bülow

Ludwig van Beethoven
Op. 79

a) It is interesting to observe how much more genius, i. e.: virility (yet without prejudice to its grace,) Beethoven exhibits in his treatment of the characteristic local note of his Viennese environment (the "Ländler,") when in the mood for employing it, than does Franz Schubert. The affinity of this "alla tedesca" to the Intermezzo of like name in the grand String-quartet Op. 130, is also worthy of note:

Op 79.   Op. 130

b) Avoid all useless time-beating with the left hand, but mark the anticipation of the dominant harmony on the third beat, which, as a peculiarity of the Master's later style, assures the connoisseur of Beethoven with greater reliability than any antiquarian researches, that this Sonatina is no "Jugendarbeit" (youthful work.)

a) The animated waltz-rhythm, in which the third beat also has a slight accent, must be brought out equally in both hands.

b) This trill is to be conceived simply as an inverted mordent with after-beat (quintuplet), and begun on the principal note.

a) The seemingly inconvenient fingering given by the Editor serves to urge the right hand to greater agility and an increase of sonority resulting therefrom; and also

b) to prevent collision with the superposed fingers of the left hand.

a) Here, as on the preceding page, the Editor has taken the liberty of giving a different shading—to promote animation in the 4-measure period, by whose frequent repetition indifference is far too easily induced. If the first 3 measures (tonic) are played *piano,* the fourth (dominant) may take an accent, in order to distinguish it from the 3 first measures of the after-phrase (dominant); the same holds good in the other case, where, by omitting in the fourth measure the *sforzato* given in the first three, the former is negatively emphasized.

b) The thematic "stretto" requires that, instead of playing 4 measures in $\frac{3}{4}$ time, 6 measures should as it were be played in $\frac{2}{4}$ time, thus obtaining a grateful variety of effect.

c) This inverted slide is executed simply thus: the rapid movement not admitting of its treatment as a turn.

Brillante.

a) This waltz, like the celebrated waltz in Weber's "Freischütz," must be executed *pianissimo* and with **no retardation** whatever; a slight acceleration in tempo is admissible.

a) This movement may be regarded as the prototype of the modern "Song without Words", and one hardly surpassed in amiable and original freshness by any.

Imagine the first subject executed by wind-instruments – say clarinets and bassoons; one measure before the second subject, the muted strings fall in, while oboe and flute alternately bear the melody.

b) The profuseness in the directions for the fingering is justified by our experience, that no player executes with finish pieces of such apparently easy technique until he recognizes them to be "difficult." The change of fingers expressly called for in places like  is indispensable for the special reason, that the "vis inertiæ" of the fingers often causes, in execution, mistaken ideas as

to the leading of the parts

a) As the passage ascends *crescendo*, the quintuplet is to be played:

b) The *sforzato* indubitably refers to the second 16th-note E♭, not to the third ($\frac{c}{a}$), where it would sound coarse and tasteless; its sharpness must, moreover, be mitigated by a preceding increase in power accompanied by a moderate *ritardando*.

a) As implied by the term "Schneller" (inverted mordent; lit. a "snap") it is well to execute this grace with a change of fingers conducive to a snap:

b) The Editor divides this passage between the hands, and therefore lets the right hand lead off:

a) All efforts toward an exact mathematical proportioning of the accompaniment-triplets to the duple rhythm of the theme, will be vain. Only assiduous separate practice with each hand will lead to the requisite independence. Compare Note (a) on Page 431 (Op. 54), where the method for practice is discussed.

a) This measure must have the character of an interrogation. The answer, with the re-entrance of the theme, must follow as naïvely as possible.

b) The short appoggiaturas must also be included in the value of the principal note, not figuring as auftakts, but thus:

Edited by Sigmund Lebert

Ludwig van Beethoven
WoO 64

*) We call special attention to these thoroughly delightful Variations because they are far too little known and appreciated. They will be particularly welcome to *young* pianists.

(a) By a comma we mark those points at which the player ought, by lifting his hands a little earlier than the note-value indicates, to bring out a rhythmical division.

(b) Proceed without interrupting the rhythm; and similarly after Variations 1 and 3.

Minore

Poco sostenuto e doloroso (♩ = 112)

Var. III

sempre **p** e legato

Maggiore

Tempo I un poco animato (♩ = 126)

Var. IV

legato

Ped. simile

SIX VARIATIONS
on the Duet
"Nel cor più non mi sento" from *La Molinara*

Edited by Sigmund Lebert

Ludwig van Beethoven
WoO 70

(a) Always strike the appoggiatura-note simultaneously with the first accompaniment - note, somewhat shortly, yet without impairing clearness. The accent falls, however, not on the appoggiatura, but on the principal note.

(b) The alterations given by us in small notes, aim at making these variations easily playable by small hands, which cannot yet stretch an octave.

(c) Continue from this movement to the following without interruption of the measure, except when the contrary is indicated by a fermata over the closing double-bar.

(a) Such a comma indicates a breaking-off somewhat sooner, and a subsequent fresh attack.

(b)

Var. II.

Var. III.

(a) Emphasize the left hand somewhat here, as it has the principal notes of the melody.

(b) Small hands must leave out the lowest tone.

Poco più tranquillo. (♪=144)

Var. IV.

(a) Both the *d-b* in the left hand, as also the *g* in the right, are to be held during the execu- tion of the small notes.

Un pochettino più animato. ($\bullet$. = 60)

Var. VI.

(a) *mp* (*mezzo piano,* rather softly) signifies a degree of tone-power between *p* and *mf*

13543

Edited by Sigmund Lebert

Ludwig van Beethoven
WoO 77

(a) and so, in general, strike all appoggiatur-as simultaneously with the accompaniment.

(b) The alterations added by us aim at making these variations easily playable by small hands which cannot yet stretch an octave.

(c) By such a comma we indicate that a rhythmical section must be indicated, and that afterwards a fresh attack must be made.

(d) *mp* (*mezzo-piano*, rather softly) signifies a degree of tone-power between *p* and *mf*.

(e) Continue from one movement to another without interruption of the measure, except after Variations 3 and 4.

Maggiore.

Tempo I un poco animato. ($\quad$ = 60)

Var. V.

(a) Emphasize the "melody-bearing" highest part.

(b) Strike *b* simultaneously with *c*

Var.VI.

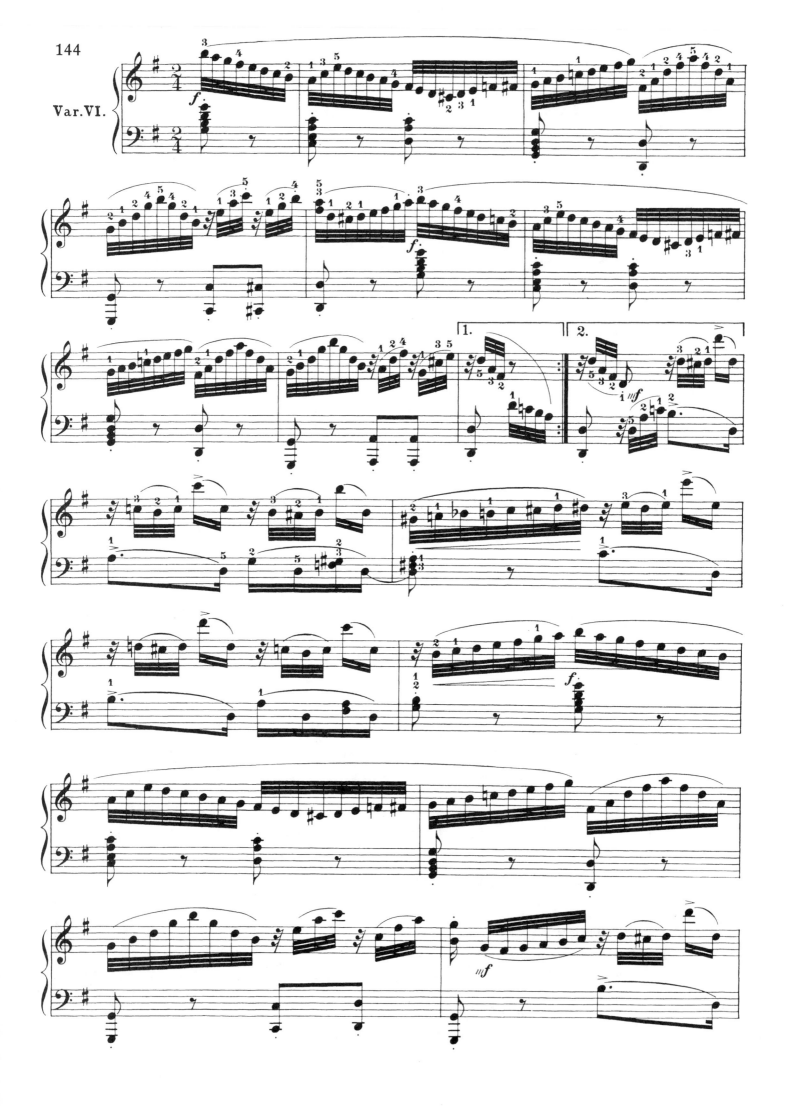

Coda.
Tempo I.

(This page has been intentionally left blank.)

Dedicated to the Princely Archbishop of Cologne, Maximilian Friedrich

SONATINA
in E-flat Major

Ludwig van Beethoven
WoO 47, No. 1

Allegro cantabile

Andante

Rondo vivace

Dedicated to the Princely Archbishop of Cologne, Maximilian Friedrich

SONATINA
in F minor

Ludwig van Beethoven
WoO 47, No. 2

Larghetto maestoso

Allegro assai

Andante maestoso

Allegro assai

SONATINA
in G Major

Ludwig van Beethoven
Anh. 5, No. 1

ROMANZE

SONATINA
in F Major

Ludwig van Beethoven
Anh. 5, No. 2

Allegro assai

166

RONDO
Allegro

BAGATELLE
in A minor
"Für Elise"

Ludwig van Beethoven
WoO 59

Poco moto

*Alternately: * *Other versions have: * * *Other editions:

BAGATELLE
in E-flat Major

Ludwig van Beethoven
Op. 33, No. 1

Andante grazioso, quasi Allegretto (♩. = 56)

BAGATELLE
in C Major

Ludwig van Beethoven
Op. 33, No. 2

Scherzo
Allegro (♩=63.)

BAGATELLE
in D Major

Ludwig van Beethoven
Op. 33, No. 6

Allegretto, quasi Andante (♩ = 56.)
Con una certa espressione parlante

(a) [music example] or, easier: [music example]

(b) as at a)

BAGATELLE
in A-flat Major

Ludwig van Beethoven
Op. 33, No. 7

BAGATELLE
in G minor

Ludwig van Beethoven
Op. 119, No. 1

BAGATELLE
in D Major

Ludwig van Beethoven
Op. 119, No. 3

BAGATELLE
in A minor

Ludwig van Beethoven
Op. 119, No. 9

BAGATELLE
in C minor

Ludwig van Beethoven
Op. 119, No. 5

BAGATELLE
in B-flat Major

Ludwig van Beethoven
Op. 119, No. 11

ADIEU TO THE PIANO

Revised and fingered by
William Scharfenberg

Attributed to
Ludwig van Beethoven
Anh. 15

Moderato, con molta espressione

TRIO

ÉCOSSAISE
in G Major

Ludwig van Beethoven
WoO 23

ÉCOSSAISE
in E-flat Major

Ludwig van Beethoven
WoO 86

WALTZ
in D Major

Ludwig van Beethoven
WoO 85

RONDO
in C Major

Ludwig van Beethoven
Op. 51, No. 1

Moderato e grazioso (♩ = 96)

RONDO A CAPRICCIO
In Hungarian Style
"Rage Over a Lost Penny"

Ludwig van Beethoven
Op. 129

a) The opus number given to this piece, 129, seems to place it among the incomparable late works of Beethoven, written in the 1820's, the final years of the composer's life: the *Diabelli Variations, Missa Solemnis, Ninth Symphony,* Late Quartets, and the *Grosse Fuge.* But, this boisterous and exuberant character piece, molded into a strict classical *Rondo,* was not the work of a mature, visionary, experimental tone poet, but of a boldly emerging young composer. It is the music of a Beethoven full of youthful abandon, perhaps even wildness, eager to gain and please a public and stake out a career, rather than the Beethoven of 30 years later, the transcendental Master, abstract thinker, and musical visionary. Accord-

ing to *Grove's Dictionary of Music and Musicians,* the piece was composed in 1795, and not published until 1828, one year following Beethoven's death. At that time, it was considered minor Beethoven, certainly not worthy of the composer of the *Fifth Symphony* and the *Emperor Concerto.* The fanciful subtitle, "Rage Over A Lost Penny" was added by the publisher, not by the composer, undoubtedly to boost sales by capitalizing on the late composer's great fame. Now, we can play it and hear it as an example of the stunning, vigorous public Beethoven, bedazzling an audience with his ferocious pianism and compositional brilliance.

The melodic thread (i.e., the rhythmic phrasing) ought to be brought out with extreme clarity;

WALTZ
in E-flat Major

Ludwig van Beethoven
WoO 84

Fine

Trio

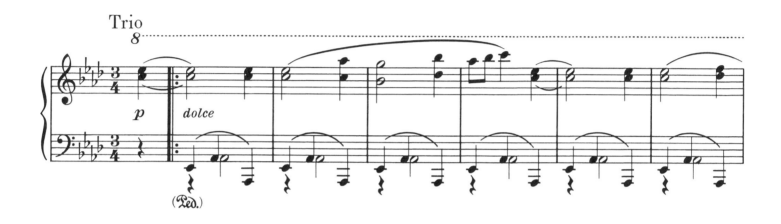

p   dolce

(Ped.)

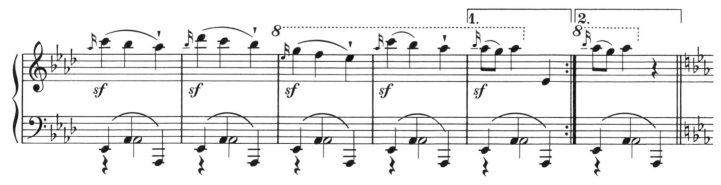

D.C.

TWELVE GERMAN DANCES

Ludwig van Beethoven
WoO 13

1

2

Fine

Trio

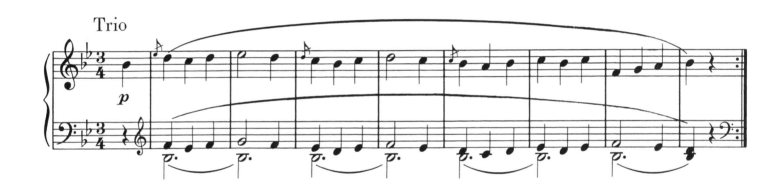

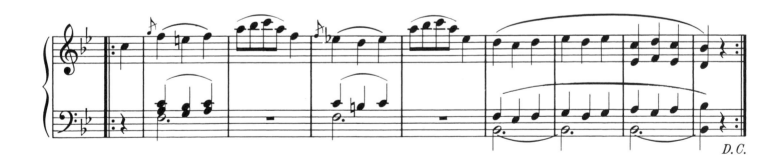

D.C.

3

Trio

Fine

D.C.

4

Fine

8

9

Fine

Trio

D.C.

10

Fine

Trio

D.C.

11

Fine

Trio

D. C.

12